EXPLORERS
OF THE
HIGHEST
PLACES
ON EARTH

by Peter Mavrikis

Raintree is an imprint of Capstone Global Library Limited, a company incorporated in
England and Wales having its registered office at 264 Banbury Road, Oxford, OX2 7DY –
Registered company number: 6695582

www.raintree.co.uk
myorders@raintree.co.uk

Text © Capstone Global Library Limited 2021
The moral rights of the proprietor have been asserted.

Edited by Anna Butzer
Designed by Kayla Rossow
Original illustrations © Capstone Global Library Limited ?
Picture research by Tracy Cummins
Production by Katy LaVigne
Originated by Capstone Global Library Ltd
Printed and bound in India

978 1 3982 0356 3 (hardback)
978 1 3982 0355 6 (paperback)

British Library Cataloguing in Publication Data
A full catalogue record for this book is available from the [British Library.]

Acknowledgements
We would like to thank the following for permission to reproduce photographs: Alamy:
The History Collection, 13; Getty Images: Bettmann, 17, Boston Globe, 23, Corbis/John van
Hasselt, 19, Paul HANNY, 27, 28, 29, PRAKASH MATHEMA, 24, Royal Geographical Society,
7, 11; Granger, NYC: AGIP - Rue des Archives, 15; Shutterstock: Hussain Warraich, 14, My
Good Images, Cover, 1, Piotr Snigorski, 5, Vixit, 8; Wikimedia: Vanessa O'Brien, 21

Every effort has been made to contact copyright holders of material reproduced in this book.
Any omissions will be rectified in subsequent printings if notice is given to the publisher.

CONTENTS

Words in bold are in the glossary.

REACHING THE TOP

For thousands of years, people have lived near the world's tallest mountains. Until modern times, many challenges have kept people from reaching the highest points on Earth. Snow slides, high-speed winds, extreme cold and the lack of **oxygen** have also stopped people from climbing. In the last 100 years, climbers have had better equipment and clothing. This has allowed them to try higher climbs.

Today, explorers around the world are climbing the tallest mountains on the planet. Learn about some explorers who have reached the highest places on Earth.

Explorers of the highest places are rewarded by seeing some of the most beautiful sights on Earth.

Chapter 1

SIR EDMUND HILLARY AND TENZIG NORGAY

Sir Edmund Hillary was a mountain explorer. He was one of the first climbers to reach the top of Mount Everest. Hillary was born in New Zealand in 1919. He completed his first major climb, Mount Ollivier in New Zealand, in 1939. After reaching the highest peaks in New Zealand, he set his sights on the highest peak in the world.

Edmund Hillary looks out over Nepal during a training session on Mount Everest in 1951.

Mount Everest

Mountain-sized challenges

Located on the border between China and Nepal, Mount Everest is part of the Himalayas. Its height is 8,850 metres (29,035 feet). Reaching the top (summit) is difficult and very dangerous. Climbers must deal with bad weather, freezing winds, snow and ice. Very little oxygen is in the air on the top part of Mount Everest. This makes it hard for climbers to breathe. It can make climbers unwell. There is also the danger of **frostbite** or falling.

A team effort

In 1953, Edmund Hillary joined a team with the goal of reaching the top of Mount Everest. While training for the climb, he met a mountaineer called Tenzig Norgay. Both climbers worked well together. They spent a lot of time preparing for the climb. On 29 May Hillary and Norgay got their chance.

Hillary and Norgay used oxygen bottles, ropes, ice axes and other climbing gear for their journey. They reached the South Summit only to find a rock wall 12 m (40 feet) tall. Not giving up, Hillary found a crack at the edge of the wall. The crack was large enough to allow him and Norgay to crawl through and reach the mountain peak.

The best view in the world

Hillary and Norgay spent 15 minutes on the top of Everest. Hillary brought along his camera and took pictures there. They were the first people to reach the highest point on Earth.

FACT

The Himalayas stretch across six countries: China, Bhutan, India, Nepal, Pakistan and Afghanistan.

Rubber walkie-talkies, oxygen tanks and boots made for high altitudes helped Edmund Hillary and Tenzig Norgay conquer the world's highest mountain.

Chapter 2

ACHILLE COMPAGNONI AND LINO LACEDELLI

Located on the border between China and Pakistan, K2 is the second-highest mountain in the world. It reaches a height of 8,611 metres (28,251 feet). Its steep drops, icy slopes, strong winds and unpredictable weather make K2 more dangerous than Mount Everest. But that didn't stop Italian mountaineers Achille Compagnoni and Lino Lacedelli from becoming the first climbers to reach the top.

Lino Lacedelli, 1954

A hard climb

Compagnoni and Lacedelli set out with others as part of an **expedition** on 28 May 1954. The team faced many challenges along the way. Fellow climbers Walter Bonatti and Amir Mehdi were part of the same team. They tried to summit the mountain first. Bad weather kept them from reaching the top. They were stuck on the mountain and left unprotected in extreme weather. It was very cold with temperatures as low as minus 46 degrees Celsius (minus 50 degrees Fahrenheit). Mehdi lost all his toes to frostbite.

K2 has only been summited by 306 people.

It took Lino Lacedelli (left) and Achille Compagnoni 64 days to travel to the top of K2.

Mission success!

Compagnoni and Lacedelli were the second two-person team to attempt the climb. The team set up their final camp at a higher location than the others. By doing this, they were able to make a final push to the top. On 31 July, they became the first climbers to reach the top of K2.

FACT

For every 20 climbers who reach the top of Mount Everest, only one reaches the top of K2.

Chapter 3
JUNKO TABEI

Junko Tabei is a Japanese mountaineer and **environmentalist**. She became the first woman to climb the Seven Summits. Her love of climbing started at a young age when she was part of a class trip and mountain climbing expedition. Years later, she broke records and reached the highest places on Earth.

Junko Tabei (left) talks with a Sherpa guide near their second camping place, still about 2,500 m (8,202 feet) from the summit.

Buried alive

In May 1975, Tabei led a team of 15 women up Mount Everest. During the climb up, members of the group, including Tabei, were buried in an **avalanche**. Luckily, all of the climbers survived, thanks to the help of their guides. After spending a few days recovering, the journey to the top continued.
By 16 May, 12 days after the avalanche, Junko Tabei was standing on the peak of Mount Everest. She was the first woman ever to make it to the top.

Breaking records

Tabei's extreme adventures did not end with Mount Everest. From 1980 to 1992, she completed the Seven Summit Challenge. Climbers who want to complete the Seven Summit Challenge must reach the top of the tallest peak in each of the seven continents. Junko was the first woman to climb all seven peaks. In total, Junko climbed 69 major mountains in more than 60 countries!

>>> Clean climber

Throughout her years climbing the world's highest places, Tabei was always concerned with how climbers affect nature. In many places, she would find rubbish left behind by other climbers. Many of her later climbs were not made to reach the highest places, but to help clean the paths for future climbers.

Tabei started climbing at the age of 10. Her love of climbing inspired her to create Japan's first climbing club for women in 1969.

Chapter **4**
VANESSA O'BRIEN

Vanessa O'Brien is an American-British mountaineer and explorer. On 28 July 2017, at the age of 52, she became the oldest woman to summit K2. She also holds the women's world record for completing the Seven Summit Challenge in just 295 days!

On top

The list of climbers to complete the Seven Summit Challenge is short. In 2013, Vanessa O'Brien joined that small group of climbers. She was the first woman to complete the challenge in less than one year.

Vanessa O'Brien on top of the K2 summit, 29 July 2017

Grand slam

Soon after she completed her 10-month goal of climbing each continent's highest peak, O'Brien set her sights on a new challenge. She wanted to travel to the North and South Poles of the planet – the coldest places on Earth. Climbing the Seven Summits and reaching the North and South Poles is known as the Explorers Grand Slam. Vanessa became the first woman to complete the Grand Slam in April 2013.

>>> Timeline of O'Brien's Seven Summit Challenge

Continent	Mountain	Elevation	Date Summited
Asia	Mount Everest	8,850 m (29,035 feet)	19 May 2012
North America	Mount Denali	6,190 m (20,310 feet)	19 June 2012
Europe	Mount Elbrus	5,642 m (18,510 feet)	15 July 2012
Australia	Mount Kosciuszko	2,228 m (7,310 feet)	3 October 2012
Antarctica	Mount Vinson Massif	4,892 m (16,050 feet)	5 December 2012
South America	Mount Aconcagua	6,962 m (22,841 feet)	20 January 2013
Africa	Mount Kilimanjaro	5,895 m (19,340 feet)	10 March 2013

During her Seven Summit Challenge training, O'Brien used some interesting techniques. One of them was attaching a lorry tyre to herself and dragging it behind to create resistance.

Chapter 5
KAMI RITA

Kami Rita is a Nepalese **Sherpa** guide. He has reached the top of Mount Everest 24 times. On 21 May 2019, he broke his own record, set less than one week earlier on 15 May.

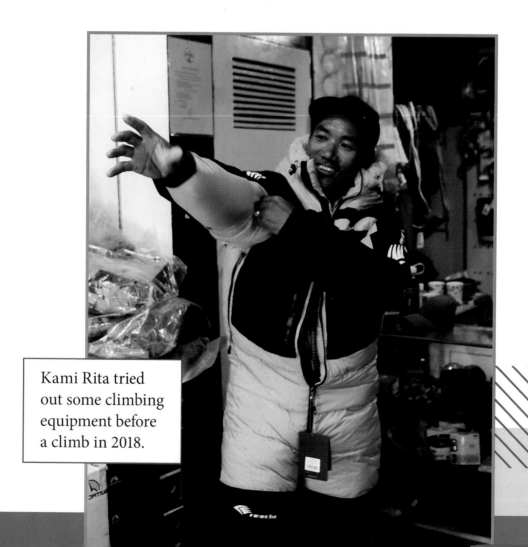

Kami Rita tried out some climbing equipment before a climb in 2018.

A lifetime of training

The native people living in and around the eastern parts of Nepal are called Sherpas. Many climbers hire Sherpas to guide them to the highest places in the Himalayas. Living at such high **altitudes** helps Sherpas handle the thinner air with less oxygen.

A dangerous job

Kami Rita comes from a family of Sherpas who have assisted extreme climbers from around the world. Kami Rita made his first climb as a guide up Everest in 1994. Since then, he has reached the top of Everest at least once a year. In 2015, Rita's **base camp** was hit by an avalanche. It killed 19 climbers. Rita always understands the dangers of climbing Everest, no matter how many times he climbs it.

Chapter 6

REINHOLD MESSNER

Born in the mountains of northern Italy, Reinhold Messner spent most of his youth climbing the peaks around him. Since then, Messner has become one of the world's most extreme explorers.

Mission impossible

Many climbers once thought it was impossible to reach the top of Everest without using an oxygen tank. Reinhold Messner, along with his climbing partner, Peter Habeler, proved them wrong. In 1978, Messner and Habeler became the first climbers to reach the top of Everest by just breathing the air around them.

Reinhold Messner, 1991

Slow and steady

With just a backpack and few supplies, they left base camp on 8 May 1978. Unlike other climbers weighed down by heavy oxygen tanks, they were able to climb quickly.

Walking, talking and even staying alert without oxygen is difficult. Without oxygen tanks, Messner and Habeler had a hard time climbing the final stretch. They used hand signals instead of talking to save their breath. They also had to stop and rest after every few steps. Going slow and steady, they reached the top of Mount Everest on 8 May 1978.

Reinhold Messner (left) and Peter Habeler were the first to climb Everest without oxygen. Today, fewer than 200 people have accomplished this feat.

Messner used an ice axe during his ascent of Mount Everest.

FACT

On 20 August 1980, Messner became the first man to reach Mount Everest alone and without an oxygen tank. He has also climbed all 14 of the world's mountains that are higher than 8,000 m (26,250 feet).

Glossary

altitude height of an object above sea level or ground level

avalanche large mass of ice, snow or soil that suddenly moves down the side of a mountain

base camp camp set up by climbers preparing to go up a mountain

environmentalist person who works to protect wildlife and natural areas

expedition journey with a goal, such as exploring or searching for something

frostbite condition that occurs when cold temperatures freeze skin

oxygen gas in the air that people and animals need to breathe

sherpa person native to the Himalayan Mountains who guides people through the mountains

Find out more

Books

Explorers: Amazing Tales of the World's Greatest Adventures, Nellie Huang (DK Children, 2019)

Mountains (Explorer Travel Guides), Chris Oxlade (Raintree, 2013)

Mountain Tops (Earth's Last Frontiers), Ellen Labrecque (Raintree, 2015)

Websites

www.bbc.co.uk/newsround/22702860
Amazing facts about Mount Everest and the people who have climbed it.

www.dkfindout.com/uk/earth/mountains
Find out more about mountains.

Index